1-43

How to
Get Up
When You're Down

Lowell Lundstrom

Read this book on your own, or study and discuss it in a group. A leader's guide with hints and helps for a group study based on this book is available from your local Christian bookstore or from Victor Books at $ .75.

VICTOR BOOKS

a division of SP Publications, Inc., Wheaton, Illinois
Offices also in Fullerton, California • Whitby, Ontario, Canada • London, England

Unless otherwise noted, all Scripture quotations are taken from the King James Version. Also quoted is *The New American Standard Bible* (NASB), © 1973, 1971, 1968, 1963, 1962, 1960, The Lockman Foundation, La Habra, Calif.

Library of Congress Catalog Card Number: 77-76353
ISBN: 0-88207-502-0

VICTOR BOOKS
A division of SP Publications, Inc.
Box 1825 ● Wheaton, Illinois 60187

Contents

1

Blessed Are the Tempted

A question often asked is, "Why does God permit man to be tempted? If God is a good God, why does He not destroy the devil and deliver me out of temptation forever?"

To answer this question we must go back to the beginning. When God made man from the dust of the ground, He created a special creature. Whereas animals were made to walk on four legs, God created man to walk uprightly. God gave him a living soul so that he could commune with God. Significantly, God gave man a will to choose between good and evil.

God could have given man a preset brain, programmed to automatic obedience, but God did not want the praise of robots. If He had, He would have been like a man buying a tape recorder and praising himself on tape, then listening with pleasure to the playback.

God created man to be sovereign, capable of choosing between good and evil, right or wrong, light or darkness, and heaven or hell. Man is able to curse or to praise God. Man is king of his own life—to do with it what he wills. However, the Word of God makes it clear that man will be held accountable for his decisions.

What good would wings be to a bird if there were no air in which to fly? What good would gills be on a fish if there were no water? And what good would a will be in a man if there were no opportunity in which to exercise it? Temptation is the test of a man's willpower.

The Apostle James, a very practical thinker of the New Testament, wrote, "My brethren, count it all joy when ye fall into divers temptations." (James 1:2) Christians are not to tremble at the thought of temptation. They should rejoice. When men are tested by temptation they are required to function at their highest levels, for temptation demonstrates several important things.

Our Superiority over Animals

God said to Adam and Eve, "Be fruitful, and multiply, and replenish the earth, and subdue it: and have dominion . . . over every living thing that moveth upon the earth" (Gen. 1:28). God obviously wanted man to live on a higher level than the animals. Man was not to be controlled by the impulses and instincts that govern animals.

A dog does not make moral decisions. A dog has no inherent sense of right and wrong. He may restrict his behavior out of fear of a whipping from his master, but even then he has no comprehension of any moral issues involved. If a dog feels like chasing other dogs, he does so without the slightest twinge of guilt—because he is a dog!

Modern teachers of human behavior have scoffed at the moral commandments of the Bible. They have said, "Let's drop all the taboos about pre-marital sex! It is not good for a man to restrain himself." This liberal idea is carried so far that many feel that "anything goes." They say, "If you feel like doing something, do it. Do it just because you want to do it. Do not hold back! Live to please yourself!"

When the issue of temptation is withdrawn from life and man follows every whim and desire of his flesh without restraint, then he is nothing more than an animal. The "false-freedom" philosophy of life is disproved by feelings of anxiety, frustration, and guilt, all of which result from giving in to temptation. Sinners are gripped by depression and emptiness. Man was not created to live without law and is frustrated until he recognizes God's law and abides by it.

Our Love for God

Jesus said, "If ye love Me, keep My commandments" (John 14:15). Temptations are tests in which we can prove our love for God. Millions of professing Christians parrot praises to God on Sunday and break His commandments on Monday. If a man loves God, he certainly will not use God's name in vain, nor will he lie, steal, or commit adultery. A man's love for God is revealed by the way he keeps God's commandments. Temptations are love tests.

God will not permit a man to be tempted beyond his ability to resist: "There hath no temptation taken you but such as is common to man: but God is faithful, who will not suffer you to be tempted above that ye are able; but will with the temptation also make a way to escape, that ye may be able to bear it" (1 Cor. 10:13).

No man can accuse God of allowing temptations that are too strong, because God will not permit a man to be tempted beyond his breaking point.

Satan's Reality
Modern man does not like to admit the reality of Satan, but once in a while, men like Charlie Manson and his hippie "family," who were tried and convicted for the murder of filmstar Sharon Tate, reveal the sinister forces of evil controlling many men and women today.

Satan was once a beautiful angel whose pride caused him to be cast out of heaven. Jesus said, "I beheld Satan as lightning fall from heaven" (Luke 10:18).

Satan unsuccessfully tempted Christ to sin, and he still directs temptations against God's children today. But remember, if God's will is exercised in a person's life, victory is certain: "The Lord knoweth how to deliver the godly out of temptation" (2 Peter 2:9) and, "For in that He Himself hath suffered being tempted, He is able to succor them that are tempted" (Heb. 2:18).

When temptation is resisted with the Lord's help,

the harmful aims of Satan are revealed and up-staged. Remember the Old Testament story of Job? No matter how much tragedy Satan brought upon this God-fearing man, Job continued to serve God. This brought great shame to Satan and great glory to God.

Our Spiritual Growth

This is why we are instructed to "count it all joy when [we] fall into divers temptations; knowing this, that the trying of [our] faith worketh patience" (James 1:2-3).

A strong man develops muscles by lifting weights. A mathematician develops his mind by struggling with equations, and Christians become strong through resisting temptations. The more we are tested, the stronger we become in God, so be happy when you are tempted. You are going to come out a better person in the end!

How have you been faring against temptation? If you have been yielding, you should learn how to find freedom from sin.

Our Freedom in Christ

Consider this statement: "For the law of the Spirit of life in Christ Jesus hath made me free from the law of sin and death!" (Rom. 8:2) Christ is the only man who ever lived without sinning and He is man's only way out of sin. Christ promised His followers, "I also will keep thee from the hour of temptation" (Rev. 3:10). When Christ is living in our hearts, we have a supernatural strength to over-come evil.

Remember, "greater is He that is in you, than he that is in the world" (1 John 4:4). Jesus said, "I will never leave thee, nor forsake thee" (Heb. 13:5). He also said, "Lo, I am with you alway, even unto the end of the world" (Matt. 28:20).

If you have been trying to overcome sin without success, ask yourself if you have given yourself completely to Jesus Christ.

Prepare for Temptation

Christ said, "I am the true vine . . . if a man abide not in Me, He is cast forth as a branch, and is withered; and men gather them, and cast them into the fire, and they are burned" (John 15:1, 6). Christ made it plain that a man will wither up and be defeated if he does not continue to abide in Christ.

It is tragic to meet backsliders who become too busy to read their Bibles and pray. They eventually drop out of church forgetting that when a person is weakened by prayerlessness, he is a natural target for temptation, finding the forces without greater than his resistance within.

Daily Bible reading and prayer is essential to victory over temptation.

Understand the Tempter

Considering the fact that many inactive Christians are plagued by temptation, the best defense against the tempter is often a good offense, "wherefore take unto you the whole armor of God, that ye may be able to withstand in the evil day" (Eph. 6:13).

It has been said of sex sins, "Some sins are conquered by fight, but immorality is only conquered by flight." If you find yourself tempted by something that is wrong, do not even go near it. When Joseph was sold to Potiphar, an officer of Pharaoh, Potiphar put him in charge of his household. Potiphar's wife was attracted to Joseph and tried to seduce him. One day, when none of the other men of the house was around, "she caught him by his garment, saying, 'Lie with me!' And he left his garment in her hand and fled, and went outside" (Gen. 39:12, NASB). Joseph left the room when Potiphar's wife tempted him.

God's Promises

Life may be a struggle but difficulties are necessary in our development toward being worthwhile citizens of heaven. Is the struggle worth the effort? Yes! The Word of God declares, "Blessed is the man that endureth temptation: for when he is tried, he shall receive the crown of life, which the Lord hath promised to them that love Him" (James 1:12).

We are promised that "if we suffer, we shall also reign with Him" (2 Tim. 2:12). Christ is coming soon to rule and reign upon this earth. Everyone who has resisted temptation will be given a Crown of Life and a share in the everlasting kingdom of God. "Eye hath not seen, nor ear heard, neither have entered into the heart of man, the things which God hath prepared for them that love Him" (1 Cor. 2:9).

We can lament that living for God is too difficult and use our lack of determination as an excuse and lose our souls, or we can determine in our hearts

to serve God, and Jesus Christ will help us overcome!

2

The Blessings of Trouble

One of the most astonishing promises of God is recorded in the Book of Romans: "And we know that all things work together for good to them that love God, to them who are the called according to His purpose" (8:28). We might ask, "How can *all things* work together for good? How can a man receive a blessing out of trouble?"

Friends

Consider how trouble reveals your real friends. You probably have a lot of fair-weather friends, but when everything goes wrong, and your character is in doubt; when you have nothing to offer anyone except yourself, the friends who really care will be there to help you while the others will fade away. You need to identify your real friends. The next time trouble comes your way, draw all the benefit out of it that you can.

A Right Perspective

Many people have mentioned to me that they became so busy with life that they did not realize how wrong they were living until trouble came. I remember the time in our own family, before any of us were Christians, when our family faced the death of my baby brother. Only then did we realize how wrong it was to live without God. Less than two years later, we had given our hearts to Christ. It took the death of my little brother to stop our family long enough to gain a right perspective.

Be careful before you blame God for the trouble that comes your way. It may be a way of helping you stop long enough to understand that there is more to life than meets the eye. After a terrible tornado struck an area in northern Minnesota and many members of one family were killed, one of the survivors said, "In one way it is good that this happened to us, because now material things do not mean anything anymore."

Sometimes when people get too busy and live without God, trouble comes along, whether it is sickness, death, or a financial crisis, and they are forced to consider the real values of life. In this way, trouble can be a blessing.

Proof of Character

Consider how trouble proves what a person really is. The Old Testament states that Job was righteous in all his ways, but no one knew about it till after his troubles were over. Even the devil did not believe that Job loved God as much as he did, claiming that if Job's blessings of wealth, health, family, and happiness were taken away from him, Job would curse God.

God disagreed with Satan and gave permission for Job to be tested, stipulating however, that the devil could not touch even one hair on the back of one of Job's camels without first receiving permission from God. God never permits the enemy to strike at us without receiving permission.

The Bible says that God will never permit sin or Satan to test us beyond our endurance. So if you have been going through a time of trouble, and you think it is more than you can bear, take heart, because your heavenly Father is watching you, and He will never permit anything to happen to you that is beyond your strength.

During Job's time of trouble, his friends were sincerely mistaken about the cause of the calamity. They thought there was something wrong with Job's life for all this evil to have befallen him. But remember, it was not Job's failures, or any sin within his life that caused the great trial; it was his righteousness and great love for God.

After the storm passed, and God had restored to Job everything that the troubles had taken away, Job must have been thrilled with the realization that he had overcome the evil one. If you overcome the trouble that comes your way, you too will rejoice in your victory!

Time for a Miracle?

Trouble opens the way for God to work a miracle in your behalf. Scripture records many instances of

God performing miracles for His people. When the children of Israel ran into trouble in Egypt, God worked nine miracles that caused the Egyptians to set them free.

When Daniel was thrown into the lions' den, God worked a miracle and the beasts did not eat him.

When Daniel's three young Hebrew friends refused to worship the golden idol, they were thrown into a furnace, but the Son of God walked with them in the flames, and they were delivered.

When the Apostle Peter was thrown into jail, the angel came and opened his cell.

When the Apostle Paul was doomed to shipwreck, an angel stood by him in the night and assured him that all on board would be saved.

If you are in the midst of trouble, you may expect a miracle from God! God is watching you even more carefully than a mother watches her child cross a busy street in the midst of heavy traffic. God will intervene either by delivering you immediately, or giving you strength to endure the trial. Remember, God has never failed to keep His promises. He says, "All things work together for good to them that love God." God does not say that everything that happens is good, but that everything works for good. Many things that happen to a child of God are unpleasant, but God can use even the unpleasantness for good when a person is committed to Him.

If Pharaoh had not given the order that all the male Hebrew babies in Egypt be killed, Moses would not have ended up in Pharaoh's court. If Joseph's brothers had not sold him into slavery, he would not have become the prime minister of Egypt. If John Bunyan had not been thrown into prison, *The Pilgrim's Progress* would not have been written. And if I had not had two automobile accidents (in which I might have been killed both times), I would not be a minister of the Gospel today.

What to Do with Trouble

Trouble has its blessings, and whenever it happens to you, you have three alternative courses of action:

First, you can blame God and turn bitter against Him.

Second, you can try to bear the burden alone until it saps all your strength and will to live.

Third, you can call upon God who loves you more than you will ever know.

The most important thing in life is to know that you are fully committed to God. Then when trouble comes, you know it is not punishment for your sin, and you will know it is not just fate or bad luck. When you are committed fully to God, everything that happens works for good.

I really pity families who are not committed to God, because when trouble comes, they have very little to rely on. A man who worked in a mortuary in Sioux City, Iowa told me that he could tell the Christians from the non-Christians by the way they faced death when they came to view the bodies of their loved ones. He said that many non-Christians would go to pieces, turn hysterical, and faint, while those who were dedicated to God demonstrated composure in spite of their grief.

One thing we know for certain is that trouble is inevitable. The best way to get a blessing out of trouble is to know you are completely committed to God!

3

When Trouble
Works for Good

One of the greatest teachings found in Scripture is that when you are living in God's will, the trouble that befalls you works for good: "And we know that all things work together for good to them that love God, to them who are the called according to His purpose" (Rom. 8:28). Notice, the Bible doesn't say all things are good, but that all things *work* for good. The Lord doesn't make any mistakes. Our heavenly Father watches over us with great concern, and we are assured that when we serve the Lord, even hardship works for good.

Joseph's Hardships
One of the greatest illustrations of this wonderful truth is Joseph. The story is recorded in the Book of Genesis, chapter 37. Joseph was his father's favorite son, and his older brothers grew very jealous of him. Joseph frequently thought of God

even when he was a boy, and his envious brothers nicknamed him "the dreamer."

One day Joseph's brothers sold him to a group of Midianite slave traders who were on their way to Egypt. The brothers kept his coat and dipped it in goat blood to deceive their father into thinking that a beast had devoured "father's pet." What greater misery could befall a man than being sold into slavery by his own brothers!

Joseph, however, never lost faith in God. Potiphar, captain of the king's guard, saw Joseph on the auction block and bought him. Notice that in these disheartening circumstances "The Lord was with Joseph, and he was a prosperous man . . . in the house of his master the Egyptian. And his master saw that the Lord was with him, and that the Lord made all that he did to prosper in his hand . . . and he made him overseer of his house" (Gen. 39:2-4).

You can't keep a good man down! Joseph, who was his father's favorite son, became Potiphar's favorite slave. He was given complete freedom to run Potiphar's household. The Lord was working the circumstances for good.

Then trouble struck again. This time it was in the form of a woman. When Potiphar's wife noticed how strong and handsome young Joseph was, she wanted to commit adultery with him. He refused and said, ". . . How then can I do this great wickedness, and sin against God?" (Gen. 39:9) When she was denied, she became so angry that she lied to her husband about Joseph's actions and he was thrown into a dungeon!

Before long, Joseph had won the favor of the prison warden: "But the Lord was with Joseph, and shewed him mercy, and gave him favor in the sight of the keeper of the prison. And the keeper of the prison committed to Joseph's hand all the prisoners that were in the prison" (Gen. 39:22).

Joseph, who was his father's favorite son and his master's favorite slave, had become the prison warden's favorite prisoner. Everything that had befallen Joseph was still working for good.

During his years in prison, Joseph continued to pray and serve God, and God gave him the ability to interpret dreams. One night the king's butler dreamed a dream he was unable to interpret and Joseph volunteered an interpretation. The butler was soon released from prison, as Joseph had predicted.

Before the butler left, Joseph said, "But think on me when it shall be well with thee, and show kindness, I pray thee, unto me, and make mention of me unto Pharaoh, and bring me out of this house" (Gen. 40:14). But the butler had a short memory: "Yet did not the chief butler remember Joseph, but forgat him" (Gen. 40:23).

One night Pharaoh had a terrible dream and none of his wise men could interpret it. When Pharaoh became angry with all of his advisors in the court, the butler remembered Joseph and told Pharaoh of the godly man in prison who interpreted dreams. Joseph interpreted the king's mysterious nightmare, and through it all, Joseph was exalted to the position of prime minister of Egypt, the greatest power on the face of the earth. Joseph became the number one man in Egypt, second only to the king, because God had worked the calamity for good.

All of the trouble that Joseph went through was part of God's plan to place him in a position of power. Joseph reached his position of influence via the slave market and the dungeon.

Soon afterward, a great famine fell upon Egypt and surrounding countries, and Joseph's own brothers came from Canaan to buy grain from the prime minister. His brothers, who had sold him into slavery, bowed down before Joseph, not realizing who he was. Joseph became the means of saving his own family.

In the same way, God will work the problems that befall us for good. Let's not give up hope! God is still on His throne and He never surrenders a man who prays to threatening circumstances.

The Three Hebrews

Shadrach, Meshach, and Abednego, the three young men who wouldn't bow to King Nebuchadnezzar's image, were threatened with death in a fiery furnace if they continued to refuse. Their answer was classic: "Our God whom we serve is able to deliver us from the burning fiery furnace, and He will deliver us out of thine hand, O king. But if not . . . we will not serve thy gods, nor worship the golden image which thou hast set up" (Dan. 3:17-18).

What determined faith! You know what happened? The king's anger burst forth, and he had the furnace heated seven times hotter than it had ever been. The soldiers grabbed the three young men, and in the process of throwing them into the furnace, they themselves were consumed by the flames.

As the king watched, he saw a strange figure walking with the three men among the flames. He cried aloud, "Did not we cast three men bound into the midst of the fire? . . . Lo, I see four men loose, walking in the midst of the fire, and they have no hurt; and the form of the fourth is like the son of God" (Dan. 3:24-25).

That's it! God did not immediately release them from the fire, but He walked with them in the midst of it. Remember, becoming a Christian doesn't mean that our troubles are over! Christians have troubles just as non-Christians do, but the difference is that the non-Christian walks through his trials alone, while the Lord is with us in the midst of trouble. He is not only with us, but He soon delivers us out of our troubles as He did the three young men in the furnace. After they came out of the fire, they were examined, and the fire hadn't even singed a hair.

The Tangled Threads

During World War II, a man was grieved to learn that his only son had been killed in action. He and his boy had been the best of buddies, and his death seemed cruel. The father's heart was broken. Under the crushing load of his grief, this Christian man asked, "Why, God, did you let it happen?"

That question was in his heart one day as he thumbed through the old family Bible and came upon a shaggy piece of cloth between the pages. Threads were hanging from the cloth in tangled confusion. It looked terrible! But when the man turned over the messy-looking tangle of threads, he saw that it was a beautiful Bible marker that said, "God is love!" That moment he received his answer. What appeared to be a mass of tangled confusion from one side was a beautiful tapestry from the other.

Life may appear to be a tangled mass of tragedy, suffering, and mistakes, but when we get to heaven and look down from the other side, we will see the workmanship of our heavenly Father and will rejoice because God worked everything together for good!

4

Discouragement

Discouragement is a spoiler and can be an oppressive trial in life. It fills your soul with sadness and bitterness. A recent survey revealed that seven out of 10 adults have flirted with the idea of suicide at some time during their lives. Even though America is the most prosperous nation on earth, America ranks seventh in suicides.

Why does a man become discouraged? What triggers the distress that sweeps over his soul? From personal experience and from the experiences of others, I have seen that a feeling of futility will cause discouragement. Futility dogs you with the question, "Are you really accomplishing anything?"

I get this feeling every time I watch the evening news or read a daily newspaper. There are so many great needs in the world and my efforts seem so small and futile. I heard a commercial the other day that really helped me in this regard. The narrator said, "You can't save the whole world, but you can save a little piece of it!" That's all any of us can do. Save a small piece of the world each day. If we do our best to serve God and help the unfortunate ones who come our way, we're doing all we can.

Failure

Futility is discouraging, but failure can destroy you. It is terribly depressing to try your best and fail miserably. I once saw a church bulletin board that read, "Mistakes prove that you attempted something." I like that. Some people never make mistakes because they have never tried anything. Remember, if you and I are ever going to do anything great in life, we're going to make a lot of mistakes—and some of them will be big ones.

If I remember correctly, Babe Ruth struck out three times for every home run he hit. Once James J. Corbett, the famous boxer, was asked, "What is most important for a man to do to become a champion boxer?"

"Fight one more round!" Corbett replied.

When Walt Disney applied at the *Kansas City Star* for a job as an artist, the editor urged him to give up his idea. Zane Grey didn't sell a story his first five years of writing. And the first time George Gershwin played the piano in public, the audience laughed him off the stage. Have you become discouraged because of failure? Congratulations! You have joined the company of champions.

There is no easy way to succeed in life. You may be torturing yourself because of a blunder you made in the past, but forget it. *Your unpleasant memories of the past are like cancer eating away at your heart!* Remember, if you are making mistakes, it proves you are attempting something. Keep on trying—keep learning from your mistakes, and eventually you will succeed, even if it's not in the field you originally intended.

If your life is fully committed to the Lord, you can count on God's help for the opportunity you would never get otherwise. The Apostle Paul said, "I can do all things through Christ which strengtheneth me" (Phil. 4:13). Pity the man who lives without God and attempts feats beyond his ability.

Fatigue

Elijah was one of the greatest prophets of the Old Testament. He was the man of God who called fire down from heaven and turned an entire nation to God in a day. But as soon as he had accomplished this astounding feat, Jezebel, the queen, became so angry that she put out a warrant for Elijah's arrest, and he had to flee the country. When Elijah finally found refuge from Jezebel's soldiers, he was exhausted. In his despair, he prayed, "O Lord, take away my life" (1 Kings 19:4). His suicidal feelings were prompted by his fatigue.

We're living so fast these days that most of us are overloaded and overworked. Millions suffer from despondency because of mental and physical fatigue. When you have "tired blood" from the hectic pace of modern life, discouragement is likely to creep in.

Maybe the answer to your discouragement is a

good rest! I'm not suggesting a vacation in which you get in your car and drive from one end of the country to the other till you arrive home fit to be buried. I'm speaking of a rest at a secluded lake or resort that will refresh your body.

God created our bodies and set aside one day out of seven for rest. When Americans turn God's Holy Day into a hectic day, they are sinning against themselves. During His earthly ministry, Christ recognized in His disciples a need to rest. He told them, "Come ye yourselves apart into a desert place, and rest awhile." The reason for their fatigue was that "there were many coming and going, and they had no leisure so much as to eat" (Mark 6:31).

You should get enough rest each night so that you wake up refreshed. For some, that might be six hours, for others eight, and for others it might mean 10 hours of sleep. But it's better to sleep at home than have a forced rest in a hospital bed.

Forgetfulness

Humans have a short memory. The Bible records the story of Ahab, king of Samaria, who had riches and great power. He lived in a huge palace decked with golden tapestries and the finest linens. A humble Jezreelite, by the name of Naboth, owned a beautiful vineyard next to the palace.

Ahab saw the vineyard and coveted it. When he tried to buy it, Naboth refused to sell. This depressed Ahab greatly and he lost his appetite: "And Ahab came into his house heavy and displeased because of the word which Naboth . . . had spoken to him . . . but Jezebel his wife came to him and said unto him, 'Why is thy spirit so sad, that thou eatest no bread?' "

Ahab answered, "Because I spake unto him [Naboth] and said unto him, 'Give me thy vineyard for money . . .' and he answered, 'I will not give thee my vineyard' " (1 Kings 21:4-6).

Ahab became depressed because he forgot how much God had already blessed him. Ahab was the king of Samaria with power, wealth, and all the pleasures of a man of his position. His servants catered to his every whim. Ahab had health and strength—what more could a man ask for?

Many, like Ahab, become depressed over the prosperity of others. Someone else gets a new house, a new car, or a new baby, and it throws many of his neighbors into depression. Someone else gets the promotion, the recognition, and many become discouraged. Jealousy and selfish ambition cause many to hit bottom. We are instructed, however, not to covet (Ex. 20:17) because covetousness robs us of our joy of living.

Consider what God has already done for you! Has He blessed you with health that millions would give a fortune to have? Has He blessed you with a family? That is priceless. Has God given you a clear mind? It doesn't matter how little you think you have, or how unfortunate you are, there are millions with less than you have. Remember that as a Christian, you have the gift of eternal life. Don't let forgetfulness rob you of your happiness.

A Lack of Faith

Have you ever seen a discouraged person about to

take a vacation? I have never seen it happen! In fact, most people on the verge of a two-week vacation are so excited they can't keep from telling everybody about it. You will see a man getting his car checked over at the filling station, saying, "Well, I guess I'll be leaving for Colorado in a few days. They say it's really beautiful out there." The psychological makeup of people is such that they become excited over a vacation.

Similarly, if we are children of the King, heirs of God, and joint-heirs with Christ, and if we are about to depart from this world for the greatest journey of all, *what do we have to become depressed about?*

Christians of years past used to sing: "There's a land that is fairer than day / And by faith I can see it afar, / Where the Father waits over the way / To prepare us a dwelling place there."

One of the first Gospel songs I ever learned had these words: "This world is not my home / I'm just a-passing thru. / My treasure is laid up / somewhere beyond the blue."

Friend, *keep the faith!* When you consider the glory that awaits you, you will find it impossible to become discouraged.

5

How to Defeat Depression

Many political analysts agree that the Eagleton affair may have cost George McGovern the presidency in 1972. Public reaction to the disclosure of the treatments Eagleton had received for depression in 1960 and 1966 prompted McGovern to drop him from the presidential ticket.

According to the National Institute of Mental Health, 4 to 8 million persons in the United States suffer from depression in any given year. About 250,000 are hospitalized. *Newsweek* magazine carried a feature story mentioning how many leaders and political figures have suffered from fits of depression. These include not only Ivan the Terrible of Russia, but also Abraham Lincoln, who had recurring bouts of melancholia, and Winston Churchill, who referred to his attacks as the "black dog" of depression. Churchill said that when this mood was upon him, he sometimes wondered whether it would not be better to hurl himself in front of a train and end it all.

You may ask, "What can a person do to defeat depression?" Many people are depressed over situations that could be changed.

Fatigue

Children cry a lot when they are tired, and when they do, parents send them to bed. Parents should do the same for themselves. When you are tired out, you have prepared yourself for a time of self-pity and depression. If you are depressed, it could be due to overwork, not enough sleep, or lack of a good diet. You might even be depressed over your weight. Before you give in to depression, check your diet, your work schedule, and your sleeping habits. Fatigue could be the cause of your depression.

Illness

I receive many letters from friends who are ill. They often write saying, "I get so depressed lying here in this hospital day after day." Pain is one of the most vicious enemies of people, frequently destroying their love for life. When you are sick, it is very important that you look to God for the strength to see you through.

Paul and Silas were early Christian missionaries. One night they were beaten and cast into prison. The Bible tells how they kept their faith in God, and at midnight they sang songs of praise. Their faith in God was their strength. God shook the prison's foundations and set them free (Acts

16:23-26). Faith in God, regardless of how you feel in your body, is the key to defeating depression.

Frustration

If you feel you are not accomplishing much with your life or in your job, chances are you will be depressed. The same old grind day after day has a way of wearing on the emotions. To maintain a healthy spirit, you occasionally need to change your routine. An evening out with friends, a change of reading habits, even changing your furniture around can do a lot to break monotony. A weekend vacation may also help.

One of the cures for depression is helping someone less fortunate than yourself. Depressed people usually seek solitude, and this is the worst thing they could do. If you become depressed, visit a sick friend in the hospital, stop by and encourage the children of a broken home, or take a few minutes to visit an old neighbor you haven't seen for a while. Take your eyes off yourself and get involved in helping someone else. It will change your entire outlook on life.

Withdrawal of God's Holy Spirit

The life of Saul, the first king of Israel, is recorded in Scripture. When the time came for Saul to be recognized as king, he was so humble that he hid behind some baggage (1 Sam. 10:22). But over the years his personality changed, and he became arrogant and stubborn. He continually refused to obey God, and finally, "The spirit of the Lord departed from Saul and an evil spirit from the Lord troubled him. And Saul's servants said unto him, 'behold now, an evil spirit . . . troubleth thee'" (1 Sam. 16:14-15).

The Bible teaches that evil spirits would like to inhabit us. Jesus cast demons out of one boy who wanted to destroy himself by casting himself into a fire. I have talked with many who have considered suicide and a few who have tried it. Most of the people I have visited realize a dark force of hell depresses them with suicidal thoughts.

In recent years, there has been a great increase in witchcraft and demon worship. The dark gloom of the occult continues to spread. The Bible teaches the reality of unseen sinister forces that depress and even possess some people. "For we wrestle not against flesh and blood, but against principalities, against powers, against the rulers of the darkness of this world" (Eph. 6:12). An oppressed or possessed person should repent of sin and seek spiritual help from someone who understands the problem.

King Saul's depression, the Bible teaches, was a result of his backsliding. Finally, God's Spirit left him and an evil spirit came to trouble him. If you were once committed to Christ but have drifted away, the best thing you could do to relieve depression is to repent! Rededicate your life to Christ and God will renew His fellowship with you.

Greed

Ambition can drive a person to despair. Solomon wrote that, "The eyes of man are never satisfied" (Prov. 27:20). It is stated in the Ten Commandments that "Thou shalt not covet" (Ex. 20:17). If someone you know is prospering and getting ahead in life and your own progress seems at a standstill, don't permit jealousy and covetousness to bring depression upon you. Rejoice with them.

Someone once made the comment that if we are not thankful for the blessings we have, we will not be happy with the blessings we are still seeking.

Referring again to the story of King Ahab of Samaria, the king who coveted a vineyard bordering his palace, you recall that he was so depressed by Naboth's refusal to sell, that his wife, Jezebel, finally devised a scheme by which she had Naboth killed. She gave the vineyard to her husband, but her treacherous act brought the wrath of God on the king and queen, and they both died violent deaths (1 Kings 22:29-40; 2 Kings 9:30-37).

If you are an ambitious person, beware of coveting someone else's achievements or possessions. By doing this you will save yourself from depression!

The life of Jacob, a deceitful schemer, is recorded in the Old Testament. Jacob deceived his father and robbed his brother of his birthright, and was forced to flee for his life.

One night, after he had fled, Jacob lay down on the ground, using stones for a pillow, and when he had fallen asleep dreamed that he saw a ladder reaching up to heaven. The glory of God was at the top of the ladder and the angels of God were ascending and descending the ladder. God spoke to Jacob and assured him of His protection. *This dream changed Jacob's night into one of the most glorious moments of his life!* God promised Jacob that He would never forsake him (Gen. 28:10-16).

Deliverance from Depression

Jesus is like the ladder in Jacob's dream. He is the means by which you can be delivered from depression.

The question is, "Do you really want to be freed from your depression?" If you want your dark depression to be changed into glorious victory, you had better use the "Jesus ladder" and start climbing now!

First, you must commit yourself to the ladder!

Anyone who climbs a ladder has to trust that the ladder will support him. Trust Christ as your personal Saviour for He is able to dispose of your depressing load of sin.

Second, you must keep climbing the ladder!

If you were once on your way up the ladder, but have been lured back down, repent of your backsliding and God will restore you.

Third, you must keep your eyes on the Lord.

I remember the old windmill we used to have on our farm. It was 60 feet high. As a small boy, I would gather my courage and climb to the top. I knew I had to keep looking up, for if I ever looked down, I would freeze and lose my nerve.

The same is true of your climb with God. Don't look down at your own troubles and don't look back at your past—*look up!* One blessing of sickness is that when you are flat on your back, you have to look up! Look up to Jesus, who is the Author and Finisher of your faith (Heb. 12:2). If you will keep your eyes on Christ you will soon escape your pit of depression.

6

The Release of Forgiveness

You will be offended many times during your life! It is impossible to live without your feelings occasionally being hurt. The question is, "What should a person do when someone offends him?" Some people carry offenses around in their memories, waiting for a chance to strike back, while others have discovered the release of forgiveness.

If you record every offense committed against you and file it away in your memory, the collection will grow into an unpleasant burden. Recently, I heard of a man who carried a grudge for 20 years! If you want to be happy in life, you must experience "the release of forgiveness."

A Parable

Peter had forgiveness in mind when he asked Jesus, "Lord, how oft shall my brother sin against me, and I forgive him. Till seven times?" (Matt. 18:21).

Peter placed the figure as high as his imagination could reach. The law required an eye for an eye and a tooth for a tooth. Revenge was an accepted response in Old Testament times. But Peter sensed the Spirit of Christ, so he ventured to say, "If I forgive my brother seven times, is that sufficient?"

Jesus replied, "I say not unto thee, until seven times: but until seventy times seven" (Matt. 18:22). Jesus said a man should forgive all offenses and hold no grudges. To illustrate this principle He told a parable: "The kingdom of heaven can be compared to a king who decided to bring his accounts up to date. In the process, one of his debtors was brought in who owed him $10 million! He couldn't pay, so the king ordered that he, his family, and possessions be sold to repay the debt. But the man fell down before the king and said, 'Oh, sir, be patient with me, and I will pay it all.' The king was filled with pity for him and released him, dismissing his debt.

"But after the man left the king he looked up a man who owed him $2,000 and grabbed him by the throat, demanding instant repayment. The man fell down before him and begged him to give him a little time. 'Be patient and I will pay it,' he pled. But his creditor wouldn't wait. He had the man arrested and jailed until the debt would be paid in full.

"The man's friends went to the king and told him what had happened. The king called before him the man he had forgiven and said, 'You evil-hearted wretch! After I forgave you your debt just because you asked me to—shouldn't you have mercy on others just as I had mercy on you?' Then the angry king sent the man to the torture chamber till every cent was repaid" (Matt. 18:23-34, author's paraphrase).

Jesus concluded the parable by saying, "So likewise shall my heavenly Father do also unto you, if ye from your hearts forgive not every one his brother their trespasses" (Matt. 18:35).

We are indebted to God for our sins and are like the man who owed his creditor $10 million; but God has forgiven our sins and erased our debt by the sacrificial death of Christ. As a result, we should pardon everyone as freely as God has pardoned us. We are commanded to release others by our forgiveness.

Those Who Trespass Against Us

Jesus taught us to pray, "Forgive us our debts as we forgive our debtors" (Matt. 6:12).

Often those who sin against us may be unaware of what they have done. For instance, you have worked hard on a special committee and the night of the big awards banquet finally arrives. The chairman recognizes everyone for their work, but he bypasses you. Your first reaction is one of shock and resentment. It appears the chairman of the project did not care enough to recognize what you did. The truth is he forgot to mention your name; it was an unintentional oversight and resentment should not find a place in your heart.

Many sensitive people are deeply hurt by others who don't even realize the harm they have done. Jesus realized this, and when He was hanging on the cross and the soldiers were making His death a mockery, He prayed, "Father forgive them, for they know not what they do" (Luke 23:34).

We should try to understand those who trespass against us because many people are still developing sensitivity to the feelings of others. Some families are raised rough and they talk bluntly without meaning to offend. Some people are so blunt with their words that they crush the feelings of friends and associates.

It is easy for your feelings to be hurt when you are young. I'll never forget the time when, as a boy, I was staying with my grandmother, and several of her friends came to visit her. They were sitting in the living room having coffee when I happened to walk in. Grandma proudly introduced me. One of the old ladies eyed me critically and said, "He sure is a skinny kid, isn't he?" Her blunt words cut like a knife, and the worst part of it was that I knew she was right! She wasn't really trying to hurt me, she was just speaking her mind.

Many insensitive people have never learned to pick their words like beautiful flowers. Some rough-talking husbands have turned their wives into bitter women. Callous, unthinking remarks hurt tender people. A country-western song describes a wife who says to her husband, "The only four-letter word you don't know is *love*."

We should forgive others their actions against us because our mood may have caused us to take offense at what was said.

On some days, a person can take in stride many things which on other days cut like a dagger.

Monday, a man may joke with his wife about a certain dress she is wearing and she might laugh and say, "Well, old baggy-pants, you don't look so sharp yourself." But if Tuesday is a terrible day and the children aren't feeling well, the washing machine has broken down, and a cake fallen flat, a critical remark by her husband might send her into tears. So forgive those who offend you. Their offense may be as much your fault as it is theirs.

We should forgive those who hurt us because they might not have intended their comment to cut as deeply as it did. This is a difficult thing for parents to handle when they have several children. The temperament of each child is different, and it takes great wisdom to know how to handle each child.

Leaders often have the diplomacy needed to correct people without hurting them, but this is not always true, and sometimes a churlish person will tear into you and hurt you much more than he realizes. Frequently, a foreman will say something to an employee that hurts much more than it was intended.

Forgive your superiors who may have hurt your feelings by what they have said. If they knew how deeply they hurt you, they probably would have worded things differently.

How to Forgive

Finally, you should forgive those who trespass against you because even if they did intend to hurt you, you are going to injure yourself even more by remembering what they did. In other words, if someone stabs you with a comment, don't let him stab you again by remembering what he said. Find the release of forgiveness. It will enable you to live without resentment.

Someone once made a fine suggestion for anyone who receives a nasty letter: never acknowledge it, never write back. If you do, the other person will know his message of hurt was delivered, but if you remain silent, he will always wonder whether or not you received it. His anxiety will be a much greater torment to him than what he said to you in the letter.

If you harbor feelings in your heart over a hurt someone gave you, the hurt is amplified a thousand times. Some people have even suffered nervous breakdowns over wrongs they could not forgive.

A close friend of mine once deeply hurt my feelings. I wasn't able to find deliverance from this event till I realized how often I must hurt God's feelings. When I remembered how many times I wanted my own way rather than God's way, and considered how often I must hurt God without even knowing it, I found it easy to forgive the brother who had hurt me.

Someone has said: "To return evil for good is like the devil. To return evil for evil is like man. To return good for evil is like the Lord."

It is often easier to talk about forgiveness than to forgive. Some people have been hurt so much that it would take a miracle of God to forgive. A man who was a prisoner in China tells how his captors tormented him without mercy. His hatred grew until he realized how displeasing it was to the

Lord. He began to pray for his tormentors and show them kindness whenever he could. Soon they changed their attitude toward him, and treated him kindly. The release of his forgiveness worked for his own good.

I heard a remarkable story about forgiveness that happened sometime ago. Though I don't remember all the details, I do remember the impression it made on me. During World War II, a certain serviceman was sent to the Philippines for duty. His faithful wife stayed at home while her husband was stationed in this distant country. While he was in the Philippines, he met a Filipino woman and wrote a heartbreaking letter to his wife, asking for a divorce.

She was crushed by the news, and bitterness filled her heart, but finally she found enough love in her heart to give him the divorce he wanted. Sometime later, her ex-husband and his new wife had a baby daughter. Not long after this, the serviceman died suddenly of a heart attack. His foreign wife and daughter were left without support and found it nearly impossible to make a living. His first wife heard what had happened and had found such release in forgiveness that she asked the woman and her daughter to come and live with her. She supported them and helped the girl through college.

Was this woman crazy? No, *she was free.* Forgiveness had released her from a bitterness which might have poisoned her. She was released from revenge and self-pity; she was released from "why" this happened to her, and was rewarded for taking such a noble step of mercy.

If someone has hurt you and you haven't forgiven him, allow yourself to experience the release of forgiveness. If God was willing to forgive you for your sins against Him, you should be willing to forgive others for their sins against you. Give up the poisonous memories filed away in the back of your mind. Surrender yourself to God and He will enable you to overcome any feelings of bitterness you have been harboring.

7

What to Do When You Don't Know What to Do

Life is fragile. One day everything is going great and the next day everything seems to explode in your face. In a moment of crisis, when you don't know what to do, what should you do? In many large cities there are emergency centers offering help over the telephone to desperate people who can call when they have no one to turn to.

Each week I receive letters from people who are going through great trials. One such letter was from a radio listener who wrote, "My main reason for writing is Mother. She went to the doctor for a checkup and was told she has a tumor. She has only one year to live. She will have surgery and further treatment. This has left her discouraged and depressed, almost to the point of giving up completely. My father was a minister, and mom and dad have been retired from the ministry for a few years. She can't seem to understand why she has this affliction after giving the best of her life to God's work."

The letter continues, "Will you pray for her at your headquarters, and also in the campaigns you conduct? Have the others pray with you. We will appreciate it greatly as it is so important to us."

Everyone can sympathize with this minister's wife who faced death. If you have been going through a trial and haven't known where to turn, there are several things you can do.

Call upon the Lord

When the Apostle Peter began to sink in the stormy Sea of Galilee, he cried out to the Lord to save him. Immediately, Jesus reached down and pulled him out of the water. During a crisis, most people call on God, but there are others who harden themselves and become bitter. I believe some circumstances are intended to teach us how to pray. When you don't know what to do, the first thing you should do is pray. If your prayers seem futile and meaningless, do your best to trust God in spite of your unbelief.

I remember an experience I had a short time after I became a Christian. Dad and I went hunting in a remote area where the ducks were sure to be flying. We drove our farm tractor and wagon to a marsh area several miles north of our home.

It was snowing heavily when we arrived and before long a full-scale blizzard began to blow in from the northwest. We decided we had better get out of the area fast before we became trapped in the snowstorm.

When we returned to the tractor we tried to start it but to our dismay we discovered the battery was dead. We weren't really alarmed until we discovered that the crank was missing!

This was a crisis! The blizzard was moving in, the tractor battery was dead, and there was no crank. The snow was blowing so hard we could only see a few yards ahead. We feared we might not be able to make it home safely, so we decided to pray. We prayed that God would put electricity into the battery. As soon as we finished our prayer, I asked dad to try the starter and it worked! The tractor engine fired up and soon we were heading home.

That night, as he tried to sleep, dad kept thinking about what had happened. It was hard for him to believe that God had helped us start the tractor. When morning came, he decided to try the starter again, but there was no charge. It was the Lord and not "luck" that turned over the starter for two desperate hunters who were caught in a blizzard.

Claim the Promises of God

Prayers are often worries put into words when they should be claims on God's promises.

I will never forget the old bus our team used to travel in before we got a new one. It was 21 years old and my brother Larry used to spend more time under it than we spent in it. The brakes were terrible and in the winter time, the bus was in such poor shape the children would catch colds from the drafts. We were crowded and miserable when we reached the point where something had to be done.

One day we were driving past the Greyhound Bus factory in North Dakota and saw a new Greyhound Scenic Cruiser MC7 parked outside. We examined it carefully and "oohed" and "aahed" as we saw the size and features of this new coach. I felt it was just what we needed, but there was one problem. The bus, without a built-in interior, cost $55,000. We didn't have $55,000, in fact, we didn't have enough money to buy birdseed for a cuckoo clock!

Somehow I felt God would provide for us if we claimed the bus for the Lord. I walked over to the bus and laid my hands on it and prayed, "Lord, somehow, someway, give us this bus because you know we need it to keep our Crusade Team on the road, helping others."

As I prayed, the Lord gave me a plan for presenting our need to friends of this ministry, and within eight months God had provided the $55,000 and the $14,000 it cost to build the interior and the extra $3,000 needed to put it on the road. God had kept His promise.

When we picked it up at the factory, the entire $72,000 needed for the new Greyhound coach was paid in full. How we praise God for the friends who prayed and the friends who gave so that our need for transportation could be provided. We also praise God for encouraging us to claim the promise of His provision.

If you have been experiencing a trial or a time of great need, dedicate yourself fully to God and claim His promise to provide for you. Praying for something and claiming it for God are two different things. Claim a promise and God will perform a miracle for you.

Consider the Cause of the Trial

The trials of Job are recorded in the Old Testament. Job was a righteous man who was highly regarded in heaven. One day Satan came before God and accused Job of serving God for profit only. Satan always says that of Christians whom God blesses. Satan said, "The only reason Job serves God is because God blesses him." The Lord knew better and permitted Satan to take away everything Job possessed except his wife and his life.

Satan destroyed Job's cattle and camels, his children, and his health. In a matter of hours Job's world fell in on him. He was bankrupt, childless and stricken with fever from the boils that covered his body. It seemed that for no reason everything went wrong; every blessing of God was taken away and Job didn't know what to do.

A lot of activity was going on behind the scenes, however, of which Job was unaware. God was testing Job's trust in Him. Heaven and hell were watching the tormented Job scraping away the residue from the boils and sores on his body.

If there seems to be no reason for your problems and afflictions, it could be that you are unaware of the spiritual struggle in the heavenlies for your life. Remember, you are surrounded by many witnesses—many martyrs who have died for the faith. They are watching you—so don't let them down.

After Job lost everything and was too sick and sore to move, his wife came storming out of the house one day and said, "Curse God and die." Her reasoning was, "Give up! God isn't good to you anymore. Curse Him and die!" But Job's finest hour was his moment of greatest depression. Job looked up and said, "Though He slay me, yet will I trust in Him" (Job 13:15). Job considered God and concluded that God is always good and to be trusted.

When the trial was over, God restored Job's health, wealth, and family, and Job became greater in every way than before. Job is a shining testimony of faith. Claim the promises of God and consider the character of God before you succumb to bitterness.

Remember, God is good and cares for you more than you will ever know.

8

Confronting Crises

Napoleon won many victories for France, and made an interesting observation about warfare. He said, "In every battle there are 15 minutes when the battle could go either way." One reason why Napoleon was so successful is that he apparently knew what to do at crucial moments during a battle when the opposing generals didn't.

If you have been confronted with a crisis in your life and you haven't known what to do, the following suggestions may help you.

Consider God's Faithfulness

When David Livingstone appeared at the University of Glasgow to receive the honorary Doctor of Law degree, he was received with silent respect. He was gaunt and weary from 16 years of exposure to Africa's hardships. One arm hung useless at his side because of an attack by a lion.

"Shall I tell you what supported me through all these years of exile among a people whose language I could not understand and whose attitude toward me was always uncertain and often hostile?" Livingstone asked the audience. "It was this promise of Christ, 'Lo, I am with you always, even unto the end of the world' " (Matt. 28:20).

Christian friend, the same Lord who led Livingstone is the Lord who is leading you. Jesus said, "Neither shall any man pluck them out of My hand" (John 10:28). The Apostle Paul wrote, "The Lord is faithful, who shall stablish you, and keep you from evil" (2 Thes. 3:3). God has never forsaken one of His children! If you will trust in God's faithfulness, it will help you when you don't know what to do.

When I was a boy, we had on our farm a big black mare that we called Mary. Occasionally she would get tangled up in barbed wire, but unlike other horses that panicked and went berserk, Mary would just stand there. Sometimes she would stand there half a day. She had enough "horse sense" to know that sooner or later we would notice she was missing and come out looking for her. She knew what to do when she didn't know what to do. Mary never harmed herself because she trusted in our faithfulness to set her free.

If you have become entangled in a desperate situation and you don't know what to do—don't do anything! Just keep your place for a while. You might hurt yourself further by panicking. God counts every sparrow that falls to the ground and He can see the situation you are in. Wait for Him as He works on your behalf. His timing is never wrong.

The Lundstrom team was once scheduled for a rally at an auditorium in Valley City, North Dakota. We arrived in Valley City early that morning for a radio interview. The wind was blowing, snow was falling, and the weather reporters were warning motorists not to drive in the area.

Soon the radio station was carrying the announcements of cancellation of school and civic events. Several asked me, "Lowell, what are we going to do about the rally?" I really didn't know what to do, so I decided to do nothing. I said, "The rally will go on as scheduled." Even a big basketball game in the area was cancelled because of the blizzard that appeared to be moving in.

Something happened that afternoon! Around five o'clock the weather began to clear up. The wind subsided, the snow stopped falling, and it turned out to be a beautiful evening. Best of all, our competition had cancelled out. We had a big crowd that evening and many were won to Christ. I was happy we had trusted God instead of the weatherman!

Commit the Situation to the Lord

In the Book of 2 Kings, you can read how Sennacherib and his Assyrian host invaded Judah. The Assyrians surrounded Jerusalem and demanded that King Hezekiah surrender the capital city. This was a great crisis. Humanly speaking, there wasn't any way out. Hezekiah's troops were terribly outnumbered!

When King Hezekiah received Sennacherib's letter demanding surrender, he "went up into the house of the Lord, and spread it before the Lord. And Hezekiah prayed before the Lord and said, 'O Lord God of Israel . . . Thou art the God, even Thou alone, of all the kingdoms of the earth; Thou hast made heaven and earth. Lord, bow down Thine ear, and hear: open, Lord, Thine eyes, and see: and hear the words of Sennacherib, which hath sent him to reproach the living God' " (2 Kings 19:14-16).

When Hezekiah didn't know what to do, he committed his desperate situation to God, for he believed God knew what to do! "And it came to pass that night, that the angel of the Lord went out, and smote in the camp of the Assyrians an hundred fourscore and five thousand [145,000] and when they [the remaining soldiers] arose early in the morning, behold, they were all dead corpses. So Sennacherib, King of Assyria departed" (2 Kings 19:35-36).

In the midst of a crisis, it is always wise to do what Hezekiah did. Take the crisis and commit it to God. If you have received a letter demanding something you haven't got, lay the letter before the Lord in prayer. That's what Hezekiah did and he was delivered from the Assyrians.

Confide in a Concerned Christian

Sometimes it is not the counsel you receive as much as having an opportunity to unburden yourself to another person, that encourages you in a time of trouble.

We often receive letters from friends who close by writing, "Thank you for taking time to read about my problems. I feel better for sharing them." It is a fact that you cannot keep your trials and anxieties bottled up inside without affecting your mental attitude and even your health.

Church problems are so complex today that the pressures on pastors sometimes may become unbearable. A friend of mine was having problems in his church. Conditions became so bad he had to find spiritual help to keep from going under.

He went to a fellow pastor and spent two hours pouring out his tale of frustration and woe. While he was talking, the pastor friend did nothing but listen. Finally, when my friend had talked himself out, he asked, "What can I do about these problems?" His friend simply said, "Fellow, you've just got to learn to roll with the punches."

These few homey words of advice, and the fact that my friend was able to unburden himself, gave him the courage to lead his church forward again.

Abraham Lincoln once said, "Be sure you're right—then go ahead!" If you have been in the valley of decision and are searching for a way out, remember what a man of God once said, "God's will grows on you!" If you are going in the right direction, God's will and the calling of your mission will grow stronger and stronger, but if you're going the wrong direction, it will become weaker and colder as time goes by.

One thing is certain, you cannot continue living a happy life if your anxieties and frustrations are trapped inside you. This is why I encourage our radio listeners to write when they have problems. Not only do our trained counselors help with advice, but they pray for needs of friends who have urgent requests. Every urgent letter of request is also given to me so that I can help with whatever counsel I can give.

There is a story in the Bible about a woman who was diseased with an issue of blood. She may have had cancer. Anyway, she was determined to reach Jesus. The crowd pressed in around Him, yet He noticed this desperate woman reaching out to Him when her hand touched the hem of His garment. Immediately, she was healed because she had reached out in faith.

I feel that each letter we receive represents a step of faith on the part of the sender. When he sends it, he is reaching out. We have received amazing answers to prayer requests that we had very little time to pray about. This is how God answers every Christian who reaches out to Him for help.

If you are facing a trying time, take a step of faith, write a letter, make a telephone call, or contact a Christian friend or pastor who will be concerned about your need. Miracles take place whenever you reach out to God.

Someone once said, "It doesn't do any good to worry, because 90% of what you are worrying about never happens and the other 10% you can't do anything about." But as Christians, we know God is concerned about the 10% situations that would destroy us.

God has said, "I will never leave thee, nor forsake thee" (Heb. 13:5). Christ is with you right now as these words become real to you. Christ is standing by you, and if you will trust Him as much as you can, you will know what to do when you won't know what to do!

9

Faith in
the Face of Defeat

As you read in the Bible of many inspiring testimonies of Christian faith, it is easy to get the impression that faith always works a miracle. This is not the case.

God's Word teaches that you can have true faith and yet not receive a miracle. This truth is made plain in the eleventh chapter of the Book of Hebrews. The Word of God teaches that faith is the substance of things hoped for, the evidence of things unseen (v. 1). Some people have the idea that faith is a wish, a hope, or a thought. The Bible states faith is a substance.

The Demonstration of Faith

An expectant mother demonstrates faith when she begins buying baby clothing as soon as her doctor tells her she is expecting. The doctor's word is all she needs to begin preparing for her baby. So it is with Christians. We believe God's Word and have begun making preparations for our eternal home.

As you read the Hebrews 11 you will continually encounter the phrase, "by faith."

Verse 4: *By faith* Abel offered unto God a more excellent sacrifice than Cain.

Verse 5: *By faith* Enoch was translated that he should not see death.

Verse 7: *By faith* Noah prepared the ark for the saving of his household.

Verses 8 and 9: *By faith* Abraham sojourned in the Land of Promise.

Verse 11: *Through faith* Sarah received strength to conceive.

Miracles Don't Always Happen

A casual reader of the Bible would come to the conclusion that when faith is present, miracles take place. However, if you read carefully the last part of Hebrews 11, you will note that "others were tortured, not accepting deliverance; that they might obtain a better resurrection. And others had trials of cruel mockings, and scourgings, yea moreover of bonds and imprisonment" (vv. 35-36).

Here we find men and women with true faith in God, being tortured, mocked, and imprisoned. Faith doesn't always produce automatic deliverance, nor does it always produce a miracle, but faith will give you the courage and the power to go through a fiery trial. The men and women referred to in Hebrews 11 had faith in the face of seeming defeat!

"They were stoned, they were sawn asunder,

were tempted, were slain with the sword: They wandered about in sheepskins and goatskins, being destitute, afflicted, tormented" (v. 37).

Friend, have you been undergoing a great trial? During a trial, a believer may muster his faith to believe God for a miracle, but when a miracle is not forthcoming, the believer grows discouraged. Yet it *is* possible to have faith in the face of apparent defeat.

Scripture states that the world was not worthy of those who were afflicted and tormented (v. 38). A Christian should not berate or belittle his faith just because he is not delivered. The Word of God says, "Of whom the world was not worthy." When a believer continues trusting and serving God during his affliction, he is defeating defeat.

Lest you question this truth, note that "these all, having obtained a good report through faith, received not the promise." (v. 39). The great promise of God was Jesus Christ and they hadn't received Christ because according to God's plan, Christ was not to be born till the fullness of time.

The three young Hebrews, Shadrach, Meshach, and Abednego whom we referred to earlier, are other examples of those who demonstrated faith in the face of defeat. God sometimes delivers from trouble, sometimes preserves us during trouble, and sometimes allows us to suffer to fulfill a higher purpose. In any case, God always compensates or rewards our faith.

You will remember that King Nebuchadnezzar made a great golden image and commanded everyone to bow down before it, but Shadrach, Meshach, and Abednego wouldn't bow. This infuriated the king and he ordered that the furnace be fired up. But the three young Hebrews still refused.

"Our God whom we serve," they said, "is able to deliver us from the burning fiery furnace, and He will deliver us out of thine hand, O King. But if not, [in other words, if God doesn't deliver us] be it known unto thee, O King, that we will not serve thy Gods nor worship the golden image which thou hast set up" (Dan. 3:18).

These men actively demonstrated their commitment to God, even in the face of bodily danger. A believer with this kind of faith cannot be defeated.

If you will believe as these men did, you will be victorious. They said (literal), "God is able to deliver us, but if He doesn't choose to do so, we will still believe."

You will remember that they were thrown into the fire but were not consumed. As the king watched, he cried in astonishment, "Did not we cast three men bound into the fire?" and when the answer came in the affirmative, he said, "I see four men loose, walking in the midst of the fire, and they have no hurt and the form of the fourth is like the Son of God" (Dan. 3:24-25).

The three young Hebrews were not immediately delivered from the fire, but they were delivered in the fire. God may not deliver you from the fiery test you are experiencing, but He will be with you in the midst of your trial.

When There's No Miracle

If you are facing a trial, always remember:

1. The absence of a miracle does not always signify an absence of faith. In fact, the very opposite could be true. I think it takes more trust in God and His purposes to be sawn in two than it does to be miraculously delivered.

2. Believe that God is able to deliver you.

3. Believe that God will deliver you if it is according to His will to do so.

4. Continue trusting God even if He doesn't deliver you.

If you demonstrate faith in the face of defeat, your faith may prompt God to intervene. But if you belittle your faith when He does not immediately act on your behalf, your faith will shrink and your joy will be threatened. So trust God and He will enable you to triumph over a depressing situation. In view of this, "Let us lay aside every weight, and the sin which doth so easily beset us, and let us run with patience the race that is set before us, looking unto Jesus, the author and finisher of our faith" (Heb. 12:1-2).

ADULT ELECTIVE SHORT STUDIES

Six-session elective studies on short Bible books and current topics. Excellent for weekend retreats, home Bible studies, mid-week sessions, Vacation Bible School, Sunday School, as well as for personal study and spiritual growth.

CAN YOU RUN AWAY FROM GOD? James Montgomery Boice gives a very warm and human understanding of God's sovereignty versus man's free will in this study of the Book of Jonah. Textbook **6-2501—$1.50**/Leader's Guide **6-2853—75¢**

FOUND: GOD'S WILL (formerly *God's Will Is Not Lost*) John MacArthur, Jr. directs a very logical and biblical discussion on how to find God's will for your life. Textbook **6-2503—$1.25**/ Leader's Guide **6-2852—75¢**

HOW TO GET UP WHEN YOU'RE DOWN Lowell Lundstrom, an evangelist, gives practical and biblical guidance on facing up to and overcoming discouragement. Textbook **6-2502—$1.25**/ Leader's Guide **6-2854—75¢**

JOHN BUNYAN AND PILGRIM'S PROGRESS A devotional classic edited by Erwin P. Rudolph. Textbook **6-2505—$1.25**/Leader's Guide **6-2856—75¢**

LIGHT IN THE VALLEY Herbert Vander Lugt takes a practical, humane, and biblical approach in this short study on death and dying. Textbook **6-2504—$1.50**/Leader's Guide **6-2851—75¢**

RUN YOUR LIFE BY THE STARS? Edited by William J. Petersen, of *Eternity* magazine. A study that looks at astrology and what the Bible says about it. Textbook **6-2506—$1.25**/Leader's Guide **6-2855—75¢**

Add 40¢ postage and handling for the first book, and 10¢ for each additional title. Add $1 for minimum order service charge for orders less than $5.

**Buy these titles at your local
Christian bookstore or order from**

VICTOR BOOKS

a division of SP Publications, Inc.
WHEATON, ILLINOIS 60187

1 · 201

57785